Happy 6th Birthday Giulia!
w/ all my love, nonna

FLORA HAS AN ADVENTURE

Karin Gertsch

To Giulia —
I wish you many
happy adventures!
Karin Gertsch

AUSTIN MACAULEY PUBLISHERS™
LONDON • CAMBRIDGE • NEW YORK • SHARJAH

Copyright © Karin Gertsch (2019)

All rights reserved. No part of this publication may be reproduced, distributed, or transmitted in any form or by any means, including photocopying, recording, or other electronic or mechanical methods, without the prior written permission of the publisher, except in the case of brief quotations embodied in critical reviews and certain other noncommercial uses permitted by copyright law. For permission requests, write to the publisher.

Any person who commits any unauthorized act in relation to this publication may be liable to criminal prosecution and civil claims for damages.

Ordering Information:

Quantity sales: special discounts are available on quantity purchases by corporations, associations, and others. For details, contact the publisher at the address below.

Gertsch, Karin
Flora Has an Adventure

ISBN 9781643781587 (Paperback)
ISBN 9781643781594 (Hardback)
ISBN 9781645367109 (ePub e-book)

Library of Congress Control No: 2019917506

The main category of the book — JUVENILE FICTION / Animals / Farm Animals

www.austinmacauley.com/us

First Published (2019)
Austin Macauley Publishers LLC
40 Wall Street, 28th Floor
New York, NY 10005
USA

mail-usa@austinmacauley.com
+1 (646) 5125767

Alla bimba
più bella del mondo!

The author lives on a Christmas tree farm in New England with her family, a Scottish terrier named Misty, and a friendly flock of chickens.

Dedicated to Elizabeth and P.G.

Without the guidance of my daughter, Elizabeth, this manuscript would not have evolved into a children's book. Thanks to my husband, Emil, for his encouragement and support. My son, Peter, and his wife, Diana, nudged me every step of the way to continue on this journey. And my grandson, Paul, will enjoy reading about the hens that provide not only the best fresh eggs, but also hours of enjoyment as we watch them take dust baths, scratch for bugs, and do jumping jacks to reach the highest beans on the poles and grapes on the trellis.

April, the children's librarian in Essex, called Featherfield Farm to ask Marge if she could bring a chicken to the Tuesday reading program. Next week's book was a classic children's story, *The Little Red Hen*, written by Margot Zemach. April thought a live chicken would add to her program.

At the appropriate hour, Marge got the dog crate from the basement and put clean shavings at the bottom. Then she came to the coop to get Flora. We girls were in our cage, and when we saw Marge coming, we ran back inside the coop. We were eager to get out through the people door. After all, it had been a long and snowy winter, and we hadn't had enough time to free range. Now it was late March, the snow had almost melted, and we were ready for spring.

Instead of opening the people door, Marge walked around the coop and came to our cage. We ran back outside, except for Flora, who had stopped to get a drink. Before we knew what was happening, Marge had closed our little door so we couldn't get back in. Marge spoke to Flora and she began clucking.

Flora had a yoga pose she got into – called a downward dog – when she became submissive. All Marge had to do was reach down, pick up Flora, put her into the dog crate, and shut the door. Flora was easy!

Soon Marge opened our little door again and we rushed back inside.
"Where is she taking Flora?" Lucy wondered.
"Maybe Flora is going to a new home?" Right away, Little Darling regretted even thinking such a thing, never mind saying it aloud.
"Wherever it is, I'm sure Flora will tell us all about it when she returns," Goldie replied.
Prima said, "Too bad Marge didn't open the door so I could go out and run around."
"Always thinking of yourself, aren't you, Prima?" remarked Tango.

Meanwhile, even though Flora had never been in a truck before, she rode along inside the dog crate, on the passenger seat, as if she did this every day. "Cluck, cluck! I'm on an adventure."

Marge talked to Flora all the way across town, with Flora clucking softly in return.

At the library, April had spread a very large tarp on the floor in case of chicken poop. Marge put the crate on the tarp and unlatched the door. Several children and adults sat around the perimeter and watched. Flora didn't hesitate and came right out. She wasn't surprised to see so many faces watching her. "Cluck, cluck!"

The children were delighted! *Well,* thought Flora, *this is fun! I'm not sure why I'm here, but I'm having an adventure. Wait 'til I tell the girls!* Soon, Flora left the tarp and walked up and down the aisles filled with books. "This is great! Cluck, cluck!"

As Marge explained several things about chickens, the children were quiet and well behaved. Then a few children got up and began to follow Flora around the library. Minutes later, everyone was up and in a zigzag fashion, with Flora in the lead. They walked around chairs, tables, bookcases, the water cooler, and several magazine and DVD racks.

When Flora got to the fish tank, she paused and tilted her head to look at the colorful fish. *Hmm. Wonder what these are?* Flora thought.

Then she continued to meander her way back to the small room nearest the entry door. Here she jumped up on the computer table and pecked on a keyboard. Flora turned her head this way and that, looking at the many faces watching her.
"Cluck, cluck. Yahoo, this is great!" Flora said.

Everyone kept quiet to see what she would do next. Flora wasn't the only one having fun, so were the children and adults!
Marge held out her hand to show everyone the beautiful green egg Flora had laid that morning; though most of the children touched it, a few were shy. Marge explained that Flora is an Ameraucana chicken; sometimes referred to as an Easter egger because of the colorful eggs these chickens lay. The children and adults asked lots of questions, and much too soon, it was time to leave.

Marge went over to the computer table and picked up Flora to put her back into the dog crate. But before she did, she held Flora so the children could stroke her soft feathers. This gave Flora a good opportunity to get a close-up look at everyone before Marge whisked her back into the crate. April took pictures of everything and said she'd put a slide show on the library's wall-mounted television, where pictures from all the library's programs are displayed for the public.

"Look!" April said, pointing to the computer screen where Flora had pecked on the keyboard. "There's a message."

Marge turned to look. "I see letters, but do they make sense?"

Everyone came closer to have a look. Flora's message was:

When Flora returned to Featherfield Farm, the hens circled around to hear her story.

"I've been to the library," Flora said proudly, as if we'd know what she meant.

"I wish Cooper, the wild rabbit who has taken up residence under our coop, were here to listen about Flora's adventure," Lucy said.

"Too bad Cooper's on his honeymoon," Goldie added.

"What's a library?" asked Prima, busily preening her wing feathers.

Flora stretched her long neck and said, "It's where people go to have fun with a chicken."

CPSIA information can be obtained
at www.ICGtesting.com
Printed in the USA
BVHW020116170120
569825BV00019B/80